KWEER KAT'S GUIDE TO
SELF CARE
NIMAL BRO

**A KWEER KAT'S GUIDE TO LOCKDOWN SELF-CARE**

Animal Bro, 2021

ISBN 9781648410819

This is Microcosm #684



For a catalog, write or visit:

Microcosm Publishing

2752 N Williams Ave.

Portland, OR 97227

**www.Microcosm.Pub**

**To join the ranks of high-class stores that feature Microcosm titles, talk to your rep:** In the U.S. **Como** (Atlantic), **Fujii** (Midwest), **Book Travelers West** (Pacific), **Turnaround** in Europe, **Manda/UTP** in Canada, **NewSouth** in Australia, and **GPG** in Asia, India, the Middle East, Africa, and Latin America. We are sold in the gift market by **Emerald** and **Faire.**

If you bought this on Amazon, I'm so sorry because you could have gotten it cheaper and supported a small, independent publisher at www.**Microcosm.Pub**

Global labor conditions are bad, and our roots in industrial Cleveland in the 70s and 80s made us appreciate the need to treat workers right. Therefore, our books are MADE IN THE USA and printed on post-consumer paper.

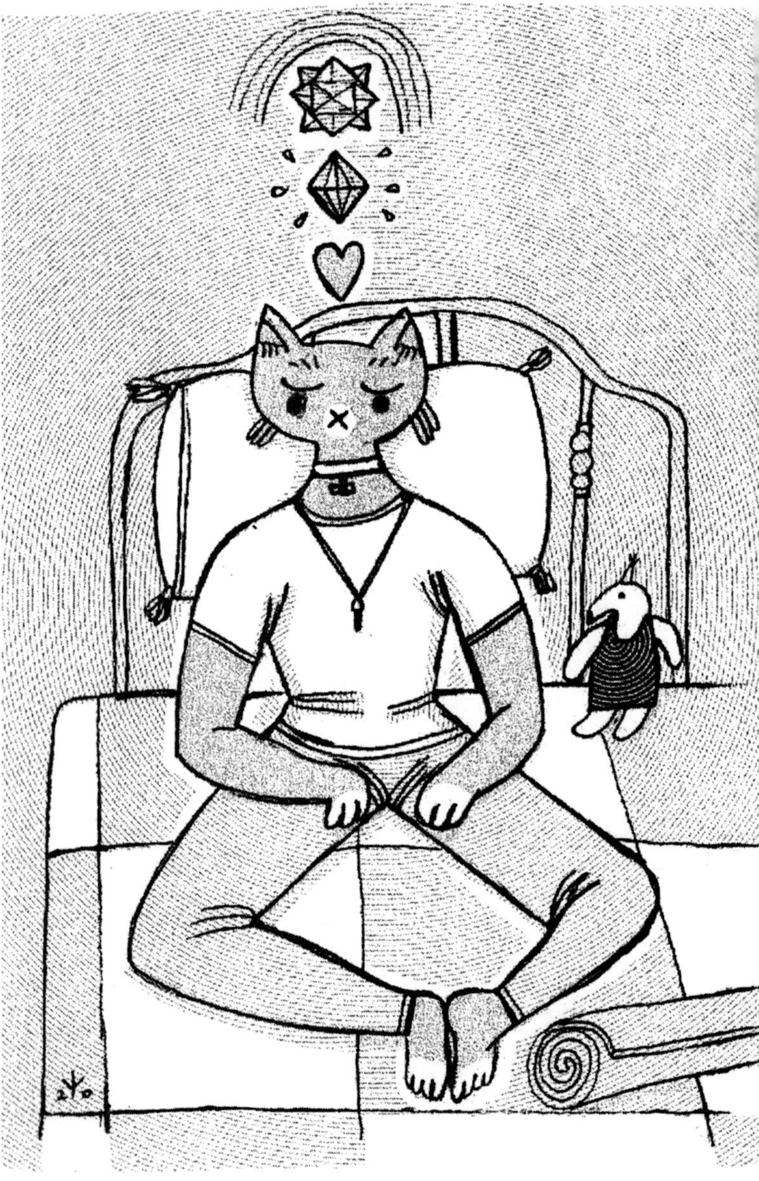

$4.95 U.S. / $6.50 CAN
ISBN 978-1-64841-081-9
US$4.95
9 781648 410819 50495>

= Contents =



@animal_bro14
animalbro.net

SKILLS TO CHANGE YOUR LIFE AND THE WORLD
www.Microcosm.Pub
2752 N WILLIAMS AVE · PORTLAND, OR 97227